Here We Come Ready or Not

by
Dorothy Stebbins Mackey

authorHOUSE™

1663 LIBERTY DRIVE, SUITE 200
BLOOMINGTON, INDIANA 47403
(800) 839-8640
WWW.AUTHORHOUSE.COM

First published by AuthorHouse 01/18/06

ISBN: 1-4208-9599-0 (sc)

Printed in the United States of America
Bloomington, Indiana

This book is printed on acid-free paper.

PREFACE

Purpose in writing this book came with the idea that many parents may not have a real understanding of what goes on in a first grade classroom. It is very easy to place blame on the school personnel without considering the whole situation. There is a lot of difference when dealing with one child at home or a whole classroom of thirty or more young children.

All names used are fictitious -- even purposely trying to not use a first or last name of any child ever taught in my classroom.

Introduction

THE SITUATIONS ARE REAL

The idea for the book came from one of the most difficult years of my teaching career when there were more than the usual number of problems in the classroom -- such as lying, fussing, broken homes, and insecurity among the classmates.

Adjustment from a very adequate classroom with twenty-three children for half a day in double sessions, then moving to a portable room and adding seven children in one day and also going a full day without water or rest rooms in the portable room. All needs of that nature had to be in the main school rooms.

Much more was accomplished in the half day with twenty-three students than with thirty students going the full day. In the half day, there was no time taken out for Physical Education or lunchroom, and more time could be given for individual attention to each child. Coming to school at noon, the children were more rested, and an unheard of PERFECT ATTENDANCE for one month with no absences or tardiness.

However, the only good thing I could say about the portable room was that there was no intercom to interrupt during lesson time, but getting seven new students in one day with other conditions in the portable was a very trying, challenging situation. Needless to say, the class got along very well without the intercom interruptions. If there was an emergency need, the office would send a child with a note to the room, which was a very rare occurrence.

Contents

Chapter Five: Some Days

Chapter Six: Gems of Humor and Wisdom

Chapter Seven: Pyschology of Education

Chapter Eight: The Way of the Classroom

CHAPTER NINE: IT WORKED FOR ME

CHAPTER TEN: THEN AND NOW

Conclusion

CHAPTER ONE

BEGINNINGS

As people were moving southward to enjoy a warmer climate, the population explosion was affecting many schools. A school in the suburb of a large southern city was just a few years old, and as the principal described it, "There were wall-to-wall children." Experienced teachers had been transferred to the new school when it was first opened, so it was considered a top school in the whole state. The enrollment each year was practically unpredictable and about three weeks after the Fall opening one year, two rooms in a neighborhood church were rented for a first grade class and a third grade class.

I was hired as teacher for the first grade class. Our room was long and narrow in rectangular shape. It was a large room with chalkboards along two sides of the room. It was to better advantage to place desks facing the long side of the room, and that way the children were closer to what was considered the front of the room. Teacher's desk which was not used very often while children were in the room was at the far side of the room.

The children and teachers were transported each day at noon by a school bus for lunch to the main school building, and then brought back to the church room after lunch. It all

1

worked out very well -- and had very few interruptions. There was no intercom making interruptive announcements.

The principal was very considerate of the teachers, and backed the teachers if a problem occurred. Often he had mentioned he felt the teachers should be "Free to teach", so unnecessary or time-consuming activities were avoided when possible. It would be good to have more principals like that now, but circumstances certainly have been changed.

As there had been four other first grade classes the first few weeks of the school term, each of the four teachers were asked to give up six of their students for the new class, and then any new students would be enrolled in my class. The students had been in school long enough for each teacher to decide which children would be selected to go to the new class. Three of the teachers sent a few of their disruptive students, but I always was very grateful for the one teacher who sent several of her better students. The one little boy she sent was reading on fifth grade level and about anything else on any level. My first observation was he should be promoted up to another grade, but the supervisor wisely vetoed the idea because she said with a "just-six" birth date and being immature, he would soon slow down in his ability -- plus needing other learning skills in math and other subjects. As the year went on, I realized she was correct in her evaluation, but it was nice when he could read any classroom material or even filmstrip captions.

One of the children I received was a little boy whose parents could not speak or hear -- known as "deaf and dumb". The child was normal and a very good student and doing very well in his school work. He had come in after the school term started, and there was a miscommunication with the parent's inability to speak. The registrar in the office did not catch the child's birth date was after the age he should be in public school. In December the downtown county office noticed the fact that he was not old enough by a few weeks for the state requirement in age, so he had to be withdrawn. This

2

happened right at the Christmas vacation. The parents then sent him to live with his grandparents in another state where he could be enrolled in school. As the Christmas vacation had started, I was not aware of what had happened until January when we were back in school and he was no longer in my room. If I had known and if it had not been my first year of teaching, I would have put up a big fuss about it. I thought the child had enough to contend with his parents' handicap and since he was doing so well in his school subjects, I thought it was not wise for him to be taken out of the school room. At times even a school policy can be altered for extenuating circumstances.

During the first month of the school year, the principal brought the supervisor to visit my room. I did not know they were coming until they walked into the room as there was no way to communicate from the office. It so happened that everything was going on in as perfect as could be for a classroom of first graders. It wasn't always like that, but at the moment, it was great and the supervisor was noticeably impressed and asked me where I had gotten my training. I know she was referring to my degree and college work, but it took me by surprise, and knowing most of my help had come from our family -- I said, "We have three children". I do not remember her response to my answer.

On my first day of teaching, as I walked up the steps of the school, I thought, "What am I doing here?" After twenty-six years of teaching, I guess I had answered my question. I taught twenty years in the first grade, and then six years in the third grade.

After the first years in the rented church room, I then was moved to the school building with a very adequate room. The buildings were in groups of four rooms in each section with a restroom in each unit. The room I was in was on the corner that faced the drive coming into the school. All the teachers appreciated knowing when the supervisor was coming for a visit. The supervisor's name was Susie Opal Sims. She tried to be helpful, but we all thought she would read educational articles and then on her visit would dwell on what she had recently read. She would swing from sight reading and not even like the alphabet letters on charts -- to phonetic reading. So trying to satisfy her observations, it was good to know when she was at the school. With the position of my classroom, I could see her little green car slowly coming up the school driveway. The other teachers asked me to let them know when I saw her coming. Her initials being SOS -- (Susie Opal Sims) -- that was the signal, or sometimes an eraser sent around to the other rooms. Without knowing the meaning of the signal, there would not be a problem if the child taking it would be intercepted.

It was interesting how she could find something to say when trying to be helpful to the teacher. One time when she was there during a small reading group, she later told me that one of the children had marked on the chalkboard back of his chair unnoticed. I thought it was very unimportant and dismissed it from my mind, but she must have thought it was important enough to mention it.-- or perhaps she was looking for something to say.

CHAPTER TWO
READY OR NOT
REFLECTIONS OF A FIRST
GRADE TEACHER

As the summer months are almost gone and school days in the Fall are fast approaching, many times the question is asked by parents, "Are you ready for school to start?" Usually my answer to the query is, "Ready or not, the summer is about over!" To most of the thirty or more beaming, shiny-faced youngsters the day just can't come soon enough. This day should be memorable, because most children never forget that 'first day of school'.

It is well for parents to avoid warnings like, "Wait until that teacher gets hold of you!" Yes, I have heard things like that, but to a child it can cause a misunderstanding. It is also well to avoid telling new students that they will have so much fun at school. It is not all fun and games. Hopefully school will be enjoyed and a happy experience, but there is also WORK, and education is a privilege -- not just some place where they go when they want to go and have fun.

READY OR NOT

"Here I come -- ready or not!" is often yelled in the child's game of Red Rover, Red Rover, let Lucy come over. Now Lucy Bryant was a petite little girl with two brothers, and she also was a tomboy, so the choosing team felt they could keep her from breaking the arm line, but knew her determination was strong in holding other players called over. At the end of the game, the side with the most children is the winner. Think of the unpopular child who is never called over and others are always called first. The worst embarrassment for a child is when always being last picked for a team -- often when there is no other choice.

Then there was the first grade student, Clark Nelson, who was registered, but for some reason his name had not been placed on any class roll. On the first day of school, each teacher was calling out the names on the roll that had been given for the class. After all children were with their teacher, Clark was left standing alone -- thinking that nobody wanted him. A kind, sympathetic teacher went to him, and said, "You are mine!", and then added Clark's name to her list. That teacher made a friend for life, and certainly made Clark's ego swell that he was "wanted".

Also, think about the spelling bees when two team captains take turns choosing their side (often with help from the other children), and of each team trying to get the best spellers so their side would "win". Here again, it is embarrassing to the least popular child to usually be the last one to be picked for a team.

These examples can be very demeaning to a child and often it happens to the same child unless there is some adult interference. If this starts in the early grades and keeps mounting through the school years even into High School with a student feeling a constant "put down" from other students, and yes even possibly from teachers unknowingly how some words might affect a child, it could give cause for some of the violent disaster revenge action to get even we are seeing in schools of today.

More and more students are learning to act out in some way to express their feelings when watching violence on television and not taking responsibility for their own actions. In these instances there are almost always reasons in the past leading up to the actual drastic revenge action.

So the question when asked by parents in late summer, "Are you ready for school to start?" I usually have felt the best answer as the children playing Red Rover would say, "Here they come -- ready or not!" Also, having the feeling many times that the parent asking the question was more than ready for the start of school after the summer weeks of having the children at home all summer. It must be one of the most exciting times in a young life -- starting to school. It is up to the parents and teachers to make it a satisfying and rewarding experience -- even though at times it could be difficult.

It is good to help the child know that the teacher and principal are the child's friends -- don't threaten with things like -- "that teacher will get you straightened out when you are in school." Yes, I have heard of children threatened with that and many other warnings.

READINESS

More importantly to the question if the teacher is ready for school is "IS THE CHILD READY FOR SCHOOL?" Readiness is such an important factor for a child as to what can be accomplished in the first school year. Many children who have been attending kindergarten already have learned to be away from Mother and home, which is a big step for some little ones. But then a little girl told me one time that she didn't go to kindergarten because she was too smart. Strange idea, but then the same child said that her Daddy has a lot of money -- "He gets $2.00 every day."

Many parents are so anxious to help in any way to get the child ready for school that there are some things better not to be stressed, but there are so many areas that are best taught before starting school. Here are a few:

1. Days of the week and months
2. Names and values of coins
3. RECOGNITION of numbers and ABC's, but NOT writing them
4. Full name, street and house number -- telephone number
5. Turn pages and look from left to right as in reading
6. FOLLOW DIRECTIONS
7. Good health and group habits -- clean bathroom habits
** 8. READ TO YOUR CHILD
9. Talk about experiences -- how can a child understand what an elephant is if he or she has never seen one or even visited a zoo

If a child is immature and just six, it might be well to consider waiting a year for entrance when the child is seven years old. Many times when talking to a parent when the child has gotten to the fourth or fifth grade, the statement has been made by the parent, "I wish I had listened to you when you suggested my child would benefit by repeating first grade or wait a year to start school. The children just referred to were not "ready" scholastically, but lawfully could not be retained in the first grade. Many times a parent feels the child would be put down for life if retained or held back for a year. However, it is difficult to understand the pressure it will put on the child and the parent in future years in trying to work above his or her ability.

THE BEST YEAR TO REPEAT IS THE FIRST GRADE -- in most cases, OR EVEN BE HELD BACK IN KINDERGARTEN!!.

CHAPTER THREE
SPECIAL HELPS

TIPS FOR BEGINNING TEACHERS

There are so many suggestions made in this area, and I will mention just a few that I feel are very important like:

1. When in doubt, ask questions and be on time
2. Be sensible and fair with discipline
3. Keep communication lines open with students and parents
4. Be considerate and get to know the custodian and secretary
5. In private conference with students, keep the door OPEN
6. Avoid any appearance of sexual "touching" criticism
7. Always be conscious of building self-esteem in students.

These suggestions are good for new or seasoned teachers.

There is a policy of some that tells teachers to never smile before Thanksgiving. Just walk into the room, throw books down on the desk and never smile. That attitude is to show the students who is in charge. That may work for some, but when a child is entering school, I feel there is a better way of showing who is in charge without intimidating the students. However, what works for one does not mean it fits the personality of others. Each teacher must find his or her own comfort zone in classroom management.

HATS OFF AND THREE CHEERS FOR PRINCIPALS AND SUPPORT PERSONNEL

PRINCIPALS

The principal and or office is really the hub of school activity. He or she can be the catalyst of discord, or hopefully an attitude of harmony in the teachers, students and parents.

Our school was blessed in having two very supportive principals. The first principal's philosophy when I started teaching was to not load the teachers with time-consuming tasks, so they would have TIME TO TEACH. He was very supportive of the teachers when parents came to discuss a problem.

The other principal had come from a High School where there had been a lot of problems -- including drugs. He never talked about that, but we all knew the situation. Our teachers felt we had to re-educate some of his ideas about teachers. Our school had been started with mature, seasoned and conscientious teachers. In the percentage rating, I would say the teachers were 99.9% efficient. It took about two years until we realized he was feeling a trustworthiness in his present staff. From then on, it was a very harmonious situation and he was greatly appreciated.

I like the story of the teacher who was called to the principal's office, and after considerable criticism by the parents of a child for receiving a low grade, they concluded by saying the other teachers were so much better and grades were also much higher -- especially the one teacher who taught Social Studies. Without the principal or teacher smiling, the teacher gently said, "I am the Social Studies teacher."

Another day the principal was sitting at the edge front corner of a desk, and said, "Sometimes you just have to stop and think things out." I did appreciate his understanding and backing. When going back several years later, a first grade teacher commented that the children today don't know how to accept responsibility. She said, "If a child drops something on the floor, they look around to see who is going to pick it up." I believe so many children are accustomed to having somebody do everything for them that it becomes expected. Several years ago children were much more innocent than children of today, and many of these characteristics have been lost and newer characteristics have been gained.

LIBRARIANS

Librarians work with all the children in the school, so are responsible for touching the lives of each child in the school, and often give the students a special desire for reading and in the selection of the reading material.

JANITORS/CUSTODIANS

There are often many undesirable jobs during the school day such as cleaning up a variety of messes that happen during the school day with small children. This is usually done with a smile and efficiency.

TEACHER AIDES

So often a thankless job, and a lot of patience needed

CAFETERIA WORKERS

Inability to suit all appetite likes and dislikes. Cooking and cleaning up. One lunchroom manager was told by the inspector that he wouldn't mind eating out of the trash can because it was scrubbed with soap and disinfectant -- quite a compliment as well as the cleanliness in kitchen and lunchroom.

BUS DRIVERS

Getting children to school safely and on time. If too strict, the parents complain. If too lax, the parents complain.

SCHOOL SECRETARIES

-- an article in a school journal was so explicit about the happenings in one day, I thought it was worth quoting, and also humorous.

8:05	A teacher had a fainting spell, but no need for a substitute
8:36	A teacher fell and smashed her glasses
9:10	The arrival of a new child who was crying. Her puppy died last night. Need to arrange for her to go home.
9:15	Child lost her potato chips and crying her heart out.
10:05	P.T.A. mothers arrive to work in the library -- they said the flag was upside down
10:30	Fight reported on the playground, but could not locate who was involved
10:45	Concerned mother called to ask if her child had arrived with lunch money

10;55	Mother called that her son had won third place in a poster contest
11:15	Grandfather brought 4-year-old to visit a fifth grade cousin, although he knew it was against school policy. Explanation needed
11:25	A six weeks order for vacuum cleaners just arrived
11:36	Telephone call from parent about policy of taking child home two hours early to go to the State Fair
11:45	Visiting school principal bought 3000 too many pencils. Wants to know if the principal would like to help sell them.
12:00	Parent upset when coming for student for the State Fair and was told it would be an unexcused absence.
12:15	Argument of two girls at office door -- one dropped a nickel in toilet, the other girl got it and wanted to keep it.
12:30	Twins reported for climbing partitions in the rest room
1:05	Lunch period at 11:15 finally eaten at 1:05
1:15	Boy came to get gauze for a boy hurt at last night ball game, and the stitches in his head had come uncovered.
1:45	Search for the school's only one auto-harp
1:48	Child reports a teacher's car in parking lot has a flat tire
1:50	By now the secretary has doctored one skinned knee, one scraped elbow, three wasp stings, and bandaged an injured hand of the maintenance crew
1:55	Picture Company called to find out if pictures should be sold on a percentage basis like they were ten years ago

2:10   Someone had to watch the children who were left after 2:00 dismissal. "Go to the secretary."

3:05   Teacher closed a window and the glass fell out

3:30   Time for a coffee break, and time to reflect on the question of "What did you do at school today?" To this question, the secretary may answer, "Oh, nothing" because no letters sent, no stencils typed, no bookkeeping, no attendance reports, no files were accomplished.

Then another day there was one teacher to be absent and sixty-two substitute teachers were called without success of getting one. So the class had to be divided and put in other classrooms. The teachers getting the extra students without warning, no doubt may have had some not-so-kind words for the secretary.

AH YES, WHAT WOULD WE DO WITHOUT OUR SUPPORT PERSONNEL?

LITTLE HELPS THAT ARE BIG HELPS

1. Lunch money -- pay for all week with exact change. If change is given to the child, it may be lost or become a toy
2. Jewelry -- child may be upset if lost and it also can become a distraction
3. Papers to be signed by parent -- return the next day
4. Possessions -- child's name on coats, hats, etc.
5. Conferences -- please limit morning conference to emergencies. Call the office for afternoon conference
6. Physical Education -- if child is to be inactive, send

note to the P.E. teacher as it is unwise to have a child alone in the room. This may be the only planning time for the teacher all day, and there may be other needs like going to the library, rest room, etc.

7. Homework -- keep stress and strain at a minimum. If stress is evident for child OR parent, STOP, take a few minutes break, and come back to it later

8. Problems -- let the teacher know. If it is important to the child, it is important to the teacher!

9. Assigned homework -- go over completed papers with the child. Purpose is for understanding what the child is doing.

CHAPTER FOUR
SO BE IT

FIRST DAY OF THE SCHOOL YEAR

Information to each teacher about prepared envelopes that contained the following

> Free lunch applications
> *Textbook rules and cards
> 3 sets of registration cards
> Receipt book for money received
> Lunch schedule
> Music and P.E. Schedules
> Substitution list
> Bulletins for each student
> *Grades one and two do not get textbook cards
> Registration cards: 4 sets are needed --

one for teacher,
one for office
one for first aid room
one for county board

ALL CARDS MUST BE SIGNED BY PARENT

Some registration cards have notices attached for lost textbooks or library books from last year

SCHEDULE SAMPLE OF ONE YEAR'S FIRST DAY FOR TEACHER

7:15 - 7:50	Outside bus duty
7:50	Children at door when teacher arrived from bus duty
	Teacher final preparation for the day
	Parents at door to pay child's donation
	Parents not at pre-registration to register child
8:18	Intercom announcement about other arrangements
	Get a count and follow schedule
9:05	Intercom again: Send a child to office with class count and
	supplemental list
9:42	Child needs help to get the rest room door opened
9:45 - 10:15	Class to go to Physical Education
10:20	Children back in classroom -- need drinks and wash hands
11:05	Intercom -- pick up information when coming to lunch
11:30	Lunch time
11:30	Lunchroom running late -- wait until called

Think this is exaggerated? No, it is actual. In all the activity, Elsie Galvin was standing by my desk. She said, "Is it all right if I cough or sneeze?" Precious child with such big concerns. It was also Elsie who was crying one day in class. I quietly asked her why she was crying. Very hesitantly she said her parents were moving. In getting more information, I found out she was a foster child, and every time her foster parents moved, she had to go to a new foster home. This information was gotten from her mother who also taught at the school, and I was assured that she had been adopted now and would be staying with them. Such a difference it made to Elsie when she was assured of her home and love situation.

Some other menial jobs that often have to be done in a first grade classroom are things like pinning skirts when buttons come off, open potato chip bags, put on head-scarves, fix pony-tails and hair clips, replace screws in desks, start orange peels, fix slip straps, tie sashes, button dresses, braid hair, and on and on. And oh, yes -- TEACH!!

On the first day of school, I often had a bulletin board with a table under it with several interesting items. Above the table on the bulletin board would be an outline of a child with real material clothing and the caption saying, "PLEASE DO TOUCH!" So often children are told to not touch anything that it did make an interesting conversation setting to the parents and children -- maybe making the child feel a little more comfortable and free to explore.

SECOND DAY OF SCHOOL

Another notice from the office
1. 8:00 - collect money and write amount paid on attendance sheet daily
2. Take up requests for free lunches -- form will be picked up by 9:00
3. Notice the P.E. schedule time for your class
4. Check lunch schedule -- may be some changes from

yesterday's time
7. Please keep 2 attendance roll sheets -- one for lunch and one for office
8. Bus duty -- turn in who you would like for your partner
9. Blue Cross rates may go up -- see me if interested

And oh, yes --- TEACH!

INTERESTING ARTICLE: PLEASE NOTICE

You may have noticed the amount of notices for you to notice. Some of our notices have not been noticed. This is very noticeable. It has been noticed that the responses to the notices have been noticeably unnoticed. This notice is to remind you to notice the notices and respond to the notices because we do not want the notices to go unnoticed.

Signed,
Department of Notification

Now this is coming from the teacher's viewpoint, but think of the work it has created in the office.

Then this note was slipped on my desk one day. The spelling has been corrected, but the content is the same. "Patrick Hough was 4 years old. He died May 10. Well, I'll tell you how he died -- he drowned in the lake. Right before he died, Patrick and his brother Jake found a shell. Last night at the funeral home, Jakie brought that shell and put two pennies in it. Then he put it in Patrick's hand and said, "Now he's got his teddy bear, and his bubble gum money." His funeral will be tomorrow." I believe this note was put on my desk by Jakie -- little Patrick's brother.

As a beginning teacher, one of the first lessons I learned was to NOT give the children an ultimatum. In my class I had an emotional disturbed boy named Lee (Short for Leonard) Fisher. As the activity level was getting a little above what I considered acceptable, I unwisely said, "The next person who gets out of a desk will have to stand by the side of the room (commonly known as the corner). Little Leo probably never heard the ultimatum that was given and he quietly got up from his desk to wander somewhere in the room. When an ultimatum is given, of course it has to be enforced. Leo stood over where he was told and began deep sobbing almost down to his toes. He was a child who tried to do what he was told to do most of the time. Ah, yes! Never again did I get myself into that situation. Somehow I graciously got out of it -- I guess by not saying how long the "side of the room" would be.

Several years ago a state superintendent summarized the job of a teacher, and in many states other duties may be added.

1. Give specialized instruction for hard of hearing, the blind, developmentally disabled, the mentally challenged, and the gifted.
2. Develop special programs for at-risk students
3. Build respect for the worth and dignity of the individual
4. Do eye testing, schedule inoculations, assist in bladder control
5. Maintain health records and age certification data
6. Attend faculty/department/grade meetings/professional workshops, and work on advanced degrees
7. Volunteer to supervise extra-curricular activities
8. Participate in fund-raising and collecting money
9. Stress the prevention of drug, alcohol, and tobacco abuse
10. Promote physical fitness and good nutrition habits - eradicate head lice
11. Inculcate morals, ethics, and values
12. Maintain order and teach self-control to the

undisciplined children of undisciplined parents

13. Provide pregnancy counseling
14. Monitor restrooms, playground, hallways, parking lots, & cafeteria
15. Discourage food fights, break up fist fights, and pray there are no knife fights
16. Develop individual and civic responsibility
17. Eliminate gender bias and sex discrimination
18. Promote ethnic and racial tolerance
19. Develop an appreciation of other people and other cultures
20. Protect civil rights, and help develop political know-how
21. Teach sex education and AIDS prevention
22. Provide suicide counseling and give first-aid instruction
23. Assist in career planning; develop skills for entry into a specific field
24. Teach etiquette and telephone manners
25. Supervise lunchroom activities, & bus duty before and after school
26. Stress bicycle, automobile and pedestrian safety
27. Keep up with the latest educational trends and implement them
28. Counsel students with small & major problems - protect privacy
29. Communicate with parents -- detect and report child abuse. Follow due process
30. Build patriotism and loyalty to the ideals of democracy
31. Develop the ability to reason, and encourage curiosity and a thirst for Learning
32. Promote a feeling of self-worth and a pride in work
33. Avoid religion and TEACH READING, WRITING, AND ARITHMETIC

MY COMMENT: If you read through all those duties, you receive extra credit for your endurance - I have wondered if the writer was aware of all that is being placed on teachers or just being redundant.

CHAPTER FIVE
SOME DAYS

ATTENTION, TEACHERS

Many days start with announcements from the office, which is usually a necessary event. However, at times they may seem like unnecessary interruptions. Especially when the day of teaching is well planned and many things are to be accomplished. Below are a few as I remember -- making it difficult to keep the attention of the class during instruction.

ANNOUNCEMENT: There will be a late bus today. Girls will be coming to the rooms to collect annual money.

ANNOUNCEMENT: Send Archie and Cliff to Speech Class. Tyler forgot his lunch box -- his mother requests him to charge his lunch.

ANNOUNCEMENT: All busses are now in
    9:00   Mrs. Smith's children came in as their teacher was delayed in getting to school

ANNOUNCEMENT: Send Mrs. Smith's children to the library. Girls came in for the annual money and to give receipts

    9:15   Marianne came in with an excuse that she had been at the dentist. An older sister came in for assignments for her sister who was to be absent today.

ANNOUNCEMENT: The lunch schedule will be changed today.

    11:00   Time for the class to go to lunch
    11:30   Another student to pick up Virgil's assignments as Virgil was absent

Announcement: Archie's mother called and will pick up Archie at the front of the school today.

Then another day

ANNOUNCEMENT: Please excuse Elsie to go to the dentist at 9:30

ANNOUNCEMENT: There will be another fire drill -- try to be out in 35 or 45 seconds.

ANNOUNCEMENT: Send five children to the library for an eye retest.

Elsie came in from the dentist with rings on all fingers -- children were very curious.

Substitute teacher in the next room came in to ask about lunch money. Lucy came in on crutches causing much interest with the children. Lucy's mother requested she have a box to support her feet as her legs were too short to touch the floor. A box was found in the cabinet, but when picked up, a puzzle and pick-up sticks fell out. Children all helped pick them up. A boy came in from the office for the attendance sheet.

ANNOUNCEMENT: The class is getting a new student. The mother was at the door for a short conference.

Virgil came in late with his father, who explained that Virgil had just gotten a tetanus shot. He had been bitten by another child in the bowling alley the night before. Please observe if there is any reaction to the tetanus shot during the day. Virgil's money for lunch was taken and a second lunch report turned into the lunchroom. Virgil had caught a butterfly and wanted to show it to the class.

The janitor is cutting the grass with a power mower outside the windows -- children are very interested and attention is on the outside activity.

ANNOUNCEMENT: I think all the teachers are here. If you don't have heat let the office know and we will see if the janitor can fix it. I think all the busses are here, so let's have a good day.

By this time the Opening Exercises on Monday are over -- lunch money, picture money, milk money, and annual money all receipted and turned into the office. However, a live puppy and a live bunny were brought to school, a roach spotted and a child suddenly said, "I love Mother and Daddy -- I do not like the debl. (Devil).

ANNOUNCEMENT: All teachers move cars for the portable

rooms to be moved in. The children of course had to stop working and watch out the windows.

ANNOUNCEMENT: Pictures of absentees and retakes are in the office to be picked up. Check the children who go to after-school day care for head lice. There has been some evidence of head lice in that room.

Music teacher came in and wanted accompaniment for Thursday morning when all the principals from other schools were to be at school for a breakfast meeting. Of course I would be glad to do that.

Mother at the door questioning why there was a note on the board the first day of school that there should be no thermos bottles. She said, "What is this about thermos bottles?" It was explained to her that they are often difficult to open, spill in the room, and MAINLY -- if they are dropped and the glass is broken, the child may think the broken glass is ice and drink it. She said, "But Cliff doesn't drink milk -- just chocolate milk." Teacher said, "Let's try it a few days, and I am sure we can work out something." Mother said, "Well, I guess we can." On the next day, Cliff wanted some milk, so I bought some for him. On the following day, Cliff held his lunch box tightly in his arms and said, "You're not supposed to see this. I don't like milk."

PREDICAMENT: A child came to the teacher and said, "I need to use the bathroom, but I can't -- my mother tightened up my pants!"

ANNOUNCEMENT: Send for Physical Education grade forms that are now in the office. Have your receipt books in by 9:30 for pictures and Children's Theater.
Fire inspector and janitor came in, "Do you have a fire extinguisher?"

Little Lee didn't make it to the rest room in time. Child was sent to the clinic and returned with a note that his mother would be there in about 30 - 45 minutes with dry clothing.

Note from the principal brought in by a child: Let Norm Kirsten sit in your room until I see if he wants to act as a sixth grader. Thanks, signed by the principal.

In February of the year, suddenly Lacey started crying each day because her mother was going to pick her up instead of letting her ride home on the bus. The reasons she gave for crying were

1. Afraid her mother wouldn't come
2. After seeing her mother, afraid she might leave
3. Cried at 8:00 before coming to school
4. Her mother might run out of gas before getting to school

ANNOUNCEMENT: Dental slips for fluoride treatment are to be turned into the office
The treatment is $1.00

Elsie had paid for a lost reader. She found the book and brought it back to school.

It involved three trips to the office about a refund.

FACULTY BULLETINS: County officials want a number of committees appointed -- choose the committee you want to be on.
1. IIF -- Instructional Improvement Committee
2. Committee to review County philosophy, goals, objectives and Math
3. Committee to formulate school philosophy, goals and objectives and Social Studies
4. Committee to finalize teacher job description and supply teacher job description

> 5. Committee for instructional model review -- in science

Daily schedule must be turned into the office before going home tomorrow.

FACULTY BULLETIN

Remember -- report cards go out Wednesday
Lunch schedule will be moved up one hour as first and second graders leave at noon
Book inventory -- I hope you are finished
Spaghetti supper -- I hope you can be here for it Friday night.
Art show -- we will send for art material on Thursday. Be sure each piece has a name tag. We will send name tags in a day or so. Additional work should not exceed 12 x 18 inches
Magician show -- take up 25 cents per child and send to office. All teachers are to come unless staying with children who are not coming to show

TEXTBOOK INVENTORY

This was planned for later in the year, but decided to go ahead and get it done now. Each grade chairman is appointed. Please meet with your chairman and request the books you want.
NOTE: All lost, abused or disfigured books are to be paid by students as follows:

> New books -- full price
>
> Used books -- ½ price

The office must have the number of books requested by 2:00

DRILLS

1. Fire Drill -- seven consecutive bells run repeatedly will signal. Take the children outside the room and stay until one long bell rings for the all-clear, or until

further instruction is given.

2. Tornado drill -- get children away from windows into the corner far as possible -- face the wall. Children in portables go to the nearest room. Tornado signal is two short rings several times. All-clear is one long ring. Tornado and Civil Defense drills are the same.

Both drills tomorrow morning.

PICTURE DAY

Children made many comments because A.J. Henry came with a suit, tie and vest for the group class picture.

Photographer took a preliminary snapshot and asked the teacher to list the names of the students as positioned in the picture. Students were called to come for the picture in another room right at P.E. time, so most of their Physical Education time was lost. A.J. Henry got something on his suit at lunch and was very disturbed. After working at the sink cabinet trying to get it off, he finally washed it off.

ANNOUNCEMENT: Be sure to keep a list of students who paid for the picture. All this time the teacher had to go to the bathroom, but had no break

(There has been no intention to assume all these interruptions and activities happened on the same day, but they are examples of things that have to be handled by school personnel. In all this, we still have to remember that the main job of teachers is TO TEACH!)

AND TEACH TOO!

As an article says it very well entitled AND TEACH, TOO! It goes on listing some of the duties of classroom teachers such as: supervising rest rooms, keep records of tardiness, records of unexcused and excused absences, fill out field trip forms, also referral and discipline forms. Make detailed descriptions of assignments for some students, return grade sheets by 1:00, schedule grade meetings before and after school, or at break. Attend faculty meetings at 3:05 and PTA meetings at night. Get detailed lesson plans to the office by 3:00 on Friday and keep up with new trends by reading professional journals and attending professional area meeting on Saturday or after school hours.

WHAT HAPPENED? I wanted to teach and thought teaching meant READING, WRITING, and COMMUNICATING with students to receive a love of the subject and desire to learn." Many politicians decide what is wrong with schools, and what needs to be done is to "shape-up teachers". This article goes on giving the time for preparation and need of more instructional time. How long does anyone think a business man or woman would continue the job with all the extra curricular involvement that is required of teachers? There would need to be considerable adjustment and continual advancement of their education on their own time, no vendors taking them out to lunch and the lunch HOUR would be limited to 30 minutes or probably less. I imagine there would soon be many who would return to his or her corporate job.

Another article that will be abbreviated here states:

When morning came, the teacher drew her children about her to teach for the time was late and much for them to learn. A decree went out that the attendance report and the Superintendent's report must be in by 12:00. After many delays, a child came to her and said, "I am sick", and she did prove that she was. The janitor and the child's mother were called. The child was sent home and the attendance report changed. Then a child cried, "I have lost my lunch ticket." The teacher cried, "I have lost my mind!"

WHY TEACHERS BURN OUT
~~ from a cartoon picture

Head: Permanent frustration from too many laws,
           social problems, bureaucrats and critics
Appearance: Hair frazzled from bad nerves
Ears: Hard of hearing from loud student exposure
Vision: Bad eyesight from filling out many forms
Stomach: Ulcer from worrying about abused children
           by parents
Clothing: Tennis shoes and tacky clothing from years
           of low pay
Posture: Sloped shoulders from bending over desks
Last picture: Teacher reading Help Wanted Classifieds

In the closing of this chapter on SOME DAYS, it has to be mentioned that all this goes on in the school rooms -- certainly not all on the same day (maybe), but it is all of necessary involvement. Our school was very blessed in having principals who were very considerate of teacher time and tried to keep interruptions at a minimum. There is just so much that has to be communicated with the teachers that it all can affect the instruction time, and I am sure that there are administrators who are not as concerned with some of the problems that are addressed in this chapter.

About any teacher can relate to most of what is mentioned in this chapter. It is said that teachers fight and lose daily uphill battles. Some reasons given are:

Too many tests, and they do not necessarily mean more learning

Too much pressure and stress on students and teachers

One of the best governors in the state where I was teaching asked the teachers what was needed instead of mandating what teachers were supposed to do.

SAYINGS OF NOTE

A battle begun is a battle half-won

A place for everything, and everything in its place

If it is worth doing, it is worth doing well

We need to learn to disagree without being disagreeable

Waste not -- want not

It is better to have it and not need it, then to need it and not have it

If we are too much in a hurry to be polite -- we are in too much of a hurry

CHAPTER SIX
GEMS OF HUMOR AND WISDOM

Out of young minds often come words of wisdom and precious thoughts. So often children have ways of saying things that unless it is written down, it would be difficult to remember the exact wording that was used. Each year I kept a class picture with the name of each child in the order of where they were in the picture. It was gratifying when I heard of a confirmed criminal with the same first and last name, to look at the picture and not see any possible resemblance.

COMMENTS OF CHILDREN

"My brother killed a bird, and it was suffering, so he killed it again."

"My birthday was on May First last time."

"What's the difference between a pig and hog?" "A hog

smells bad."

"I bet I don't get through with my work. If I don't, I'll have a hernia! That's what my daddy says."

Girl describing a pre-primer story - "It has a 1,000 jumps in it."

(Boy)- "Aren't we supposed to love everyone? She said she didn't love me. She said she loved everyone in here except me."

Then Lucy sent a folded note to Henry that said, "I love you, Henry I have me heart set on you."

"We're going to move because down in the basement behind the furnace there is a 'For Sale' sign."

Child brought some bird seed for science class. Another child wanted to know if we were going to plant birds.

"Is your mama mean?" "Some of the time, but not all the time."

(Boy)- "I always think about girls -- all my dreams are about girls. They always want to kiss you." "My father fights my mother "(Got down on the floor and showed us.)

"My mother didn't get my hair part even with my nose."

"What is a grouch?" (Answer)- That's where you keep a car."

Rhyming words: Mary had a little lamb, etc. "What does 'fleece' mean?" "That's the black little things that get on dogs."

"I cost 49 pounds."

My mother sells perfume, and she is assistant to President Clinton. Yes, she assists President Clinton. She doesn't work in a store, but goes in a car and sells perfume, and assists President Clinton."

Virgil said, "It is a rumor that the principal has an electric paddle." If he uses it on me, we can sue him -- my grandmother said so. We can sue if it makes a blue mark -- we can sue.

"I was born on the beach by some water. I was sitting in the water with a diaper on."

"My daddy has money -- he gets $2.00 every day."

(Boy to girl) - "You are so fat -- I like you."

A very conscientious boy had a careless paper and did it over. He returned and sweetly said, "I am sorry you had to go to the trouble with me."

"I feel sick to my stomach, but what does that mean? My mother says that."

"What are we supposed to do after we're through doing what we are supposed to do next?"

Little boy came from recess with his shirt pulled up and bare stomach sticking out. The child explained that his stomach hurt, and the principal asked him "to try to stick it out until noon".

"One time my grandfather was smoking, and we had to go to the funeral."

"Cliff said a bad word that only big people can say."

"My sister has the chicken pops; my mother thinks my brother is five."

Boy said he throws his clothes on the floor, and his baby sister puts them in the commode and then flushes them down. "It gets expensive, but the clothes get washed."

"I am having my first date -- I am going out to eat with my friend girl."

While reading a child was helped with the word 'thank'. Again she had trouble with the word and said, "I'm thanking, I'm thanking."

When studying the desert, the children were asked to bring in something about the desert. Next day a child brought in some cake and said he was to bring in some dessert to share.

A DISRUPTIVE STUDENT

In my many years of teaching, there is one child who stands out in my mind as a very difficult, maladjusted boy. I will call him Virgil Cottrell. Mainly a lot of his problem was caused by his mother who could not seem to admit her son had any problems. Most of Virgil's misbehavior was excused by his mother for one reason or another -- usually blaming it on the school personnel. Toward the end of the year, I think the message was getting to her that there was a problem that needed to be corrected, because her notes had a different tone than the ones at the first of the year. The boy was now in the third grade and had a very definite reputation that had come with him since he was in kindergarten.

A note written by the second grade teacher was that Virgil's father would not agree to his being retained in second grade even though he was doing low satisfactory work -- he was immature and if the child were the teacher's son, she would want him in a comfortable learning position the next year. The mother agreed with the second grade teacher, but the father would never agree to holding him back. There were so many confrontations with the other children. To summarize the situation, a report that was sent to an evaluator in the guidance department concerning Virgil and explain his problem is as follows:

In the first few weeks of the school year, I was pleased with Virgil's progress with adjustment to a new grade, teacher and classmates. Virgil had some problems with the other children, but I felt they had been handled in a satisfactory manner and for his benefit. To my surprise after three weeks of school Virgil's mother requested a conference with the principal and teacher, suggesting there were unfair methods of discipline used. For this reason I am listing some of the situations as examples.

1. Virgil's mother has said he felt embarrassed to have his desk at the front of the room (He was in the first seat, second row from the windows to receive individual help and also so he could function there better.)
2. Mrs. Cottrell didn't think Virgil should have to stand

outside the room by himself (Virgil came into the room yelling loudly about some other children. Others were involved, but Virgil was the only one yelling. He was told to go outside and get himself under control, and then come into the room. He stood about a minute, came in, and we talked out the problem in a calm manner.

3. Virgil was asking to use the rest room quite frequently and then playing in the rest room bothering the other children coming in. In October, his mother was asked if it was necessary for him to make so many trips to the rest room. She answered in a note, "I really don't think he needs to go as often as he is going." Then on December 5, when Virgil had been to the rest room several times during the morning already, he wanted to go again and his request was denied. He then wet his pants in the room and in a LOUD VOICE announced what he had done to the whole class.

A note came from his mother concerning this and requested a transfer to another room saying, "....under no circumstances should Virgil be denied or any other child the privilege of going to the rest room. The humiliation alone, of using your pants in front of your peers is more than children can cope with." On December 7, when again the trips started every ten or fifteen minutes and was told the teacher thought it was not necessary, he YELLED back, "My mother said she sent you a note to let me use the rest room whenever I wanted to."

There are so many other instances that come to my mind, but to sum up I would describe Virgil as good-looking, a capable child with frustrations from a lack of social and emotional maturity which made it extremely difficult to adjust to a regular class situation. As his teacher, I felt handicapped to help him with a lack of backing from home. He was impulsive, aggressive, angered quickly, hostile and sometimes could not sit still. There were always excuses coming from home for his actions or when he had not finished his homework. One time he told his teacher that he did not like the word "gentleman" -- he liked "get down and get dirty." It appeared he had a low self-complex of himself and on an assignment of writing a letter, he addressed it to Miss Mud from Mr. Mud.

Often I have wondered what the future held for Virgil. In the fourth Grade, the Guidance Department got involved as to placing him in a special class. His mother wanted him to be taught the major subjects by a teacher in the High School because she thought he was so advanced. He had all F's in subjects in the fourth grade and wouldn't even put his name on his paper. So his reputation went along with him, and as our principal said, "You can't win them all."

CHAPTER SEVEN
PSYCHOLOGY OF EDUCATION

Most teachers remember instances that happened in the classroom when it was a blessing that there was not an immediate response taken to the action of a child. Immediately, I think of one time concerning Tyler Nickerson, who was a very large, lovable first grader with several unavoidable undesirable unsocial habits. During a small reading group, Lucy Bryant (who was usually a helpful and very considerate little girl), picked up something from the floor and put it on Tyler's forehead. My first impulse was to question her action, but in my hesitation, she smiled at Tyler and we all saw a small gold star that had been dropped on the floor that was now on Tyler's forehead. When Tyler realized what it was, he beamed with delight. This brought tears to my eyes and also to some of the eyes of the children. My interference as the teacher could have spoiled the whole incident.

As a cartoon of Beetle Bailey once showed Beetle telling the secretary that at last the old man liked one of his reports, and look what he gave me! The secretary responded, "A little star on your forehead?" Then Beetle laughingly said, "I haven't had one of those since the third grade!" Little things do mean a lot -- and especially to children.

At an early age, children become sensitive to the emotional and physical needs of other children if they are guided in that direction at home and school. All of my classes soon learned that making fun or laughing at a child would NOT be tolerated. I told them we could get anyone in the room (including the teacher), and find something to laugh at about them. That seemed to remedy a lot of situations and NEVER had to do it, and probably never would have done it, but it did seem to help discourage any problem along that line.

There were times in my years of teaching that there would be an occurrence usually involving one or more children that I almost felt helpless as to a solution. After an unspoken two-second silent prayer -- "Please help me!" -- a PERFECT ANSWER would come -- might be called a silent "breath prayer". I always felt confident the answer came from a Divine source. -- "Thank You, Father". There was an article I read of how to use a spiritual intelligence that I thought expressed it well by saying that when a person reaches beyond reason to a deeper level of understanding, it would be considered usually involving help from the Holy Spirit.

It can start in the early grades and can keep mounting through Elementary School on into High School that a student can constantly feel a "put down" from other students -- and yes, even sometimes from teachers who unknowingly do not realize how some words can effect a child. It can give cause for some of the violent drastic actions we see in the schools, as more and more students learn to express their feelings -- some by seeing the violence on television and not willing to take responsibility for their own actions. In these instances there is almost always something in the student's life leading up to the actual drastic response.

Dear God, education can be a mockery if Your name cannot be mentioned as we are to train young students for life and not mention the name of Jesus who IS life.

A poem by Helen Keller that I have thought was very meaningful --

They took away what should have been my eyes,
(But I remembered Milton's Paradise).
They took away what should have been my ears,
(Beethoven came and wiped away my tears).
They took away what should have been my tongue,
(But I had talked with God when I was young).
He would not let them take away my soul --
Possessing that, I still possess the whole.

SELF ESTEEM

It is SO important to build the value in a child's life by parents, teachers, and other acquaintances. I have been told that a flock of geese will encourage the leader by honking as they fly. If one goose tires and drops out of the flock, several other geese will also drop out to stay with the tiring one until they all can go together to rejoin the other geese.

As an example in my own life -- we had a kindergarten rhythm band. It seemed to me that I was almost always given the sticks to play, even though there was an accordion, cymbals, drum, xylophone, and other instruments. Most of the children got sticks to play, and would sit on the floor in front of the other players. So to me, I thought the teacher felt I was not able to play anything other than sticks. I know now there were other reasons, and usually the boys got the other instruments. This is to say that even the little things can be taken by a child in a "put-down" feeling.

Often it is heard that parents say they would do things differently now than they did at the time of their young child's life. One parent I heard say that there would be more finger-painting and less finger pointing, more hugging and less tugging. They would build self-esteem first and the house later, be firm less often, and affirm much more. It is a fact that children who come from homes that are structured, but the children given some permissiveness without reason -- show more creativity.

CLASS MANAGEMENT

Many schools send classroom guidelines to the home at the beginning of the school year, so if they are read by parents there is a better understanding of the school policies. One school said rules must be made to protect persons, property, and the educational program. The rules must be reasonable, enforceable and legal.

Another school gave the school policy on cheating, office availability, telephones, tardiness, truancy, respect for teacher, drugs, tobacco, visitors, suspension, make-up work, dress requirements, parental responsibility, fire drills, tornado drills, faculty, etc. It seemed very well explained in each category and certainly should avoid any future misunderstanding by parents in the way situations were handled. In the "Talk with Teacher" night, I usually told parents that if there was something about the child I needed to know, or if they would like a conference, please send a note giving a convenient time for me to call in the evening. I explained that I also had a family and was very conscious of family time, but if a child was upset about something that came up at school, I wanted to know about it.

CLASSROOM DISCIPLINE

It is a big help to let the students make rules and that all must abide by them. Some little things often work by stopping, and look at the child who is not behaving until the behavior has improved. Other tips like putting a hand on the shoulder of a child while continuing the lesson, or stop the lesson abruptly, everybody stand up and sing or do a few stretch exercises. Organizing the class by giving children responsibilities works well like: leading the class to lunch, P.E., Music, or whenever leaving the room. This should be a different leader for each activity. I chose to let the same leader most of the year as that was his or her responsibility. Other jobs could be cleaning off the lunch room tables, turning on and off lights when leaving or entering the room, and many other jobs. In some classes, it might be better to rotate the jobs so every child feels needed.

When the class seems to start getting dull, I found it helpful to move all the furniture around. This just to be done occasionally, of course -- like once every six weeks. Some years as needed I moved the desk once a week by having the child in the last desk in the row move to the front desk, and all other move back one desk. Change seems to add energy, life and vigor.

On this subject of self-esteem, I came across an article that so impressed me that I gave a copy of it to each of my student teachers. For that reason I am including the article in its entirety. (All I know is the author's name, so cannot give any other credit than that, other than it was written in the NEA Journal - September, 1965.

THE RED SWEATER by E. Jean Jessop

The children left for school and the house was quiet with a soft rain on the roof. I sat on the attic floor holding the red sweater that had been tucked away with my old book reports and Brownie pins in the bottom of the trunk. Forgotten was why I was up here, but I found myself swept away by the hurt and indignity of a long-ago day in the third grade.

That day I had a fried egg sandwich in my lunch. I didn't like fried egg sandwiches, but I almost always had them. Mrs.

Moody, our housekeeper, said they were nourishing and she could just as well fry up an extra egg at breakfast than fussing around with special stuff that only spoiled a child. We had a housekeeper because my mother was in a TB sanatorium.

"I wonder what TB really is," I thought. Maybe I could ask our teacher, Miss Fortin. It must be something they haven't told me about because grown-ups give you a funny look when you say that's where your mother is -- like they wish you hadn't mentioned it and they won't tell anyone.

The bell rang to line up after lunch. I got near the end of the line to stay away from this big, fresh girl in our room who liked to pick on some of the kids -- especially me. She used to pull my braids and sometimes she'd stomp on my shoes. When I got home, Mrs. Moody would yell at me for getting my shoes all scuffed up. Then Daddy would look sad and tell me to try not to make Mrs. Moody mad because it was hard to get a housekeeper out in the country where we lived. If Mrs. Moody got too mad and quit, he said that I would have to go live with Aunt Sarah in the city because he couldn't look after me by myself.

Miss Fortin wasn't at the head of our line. Instead there was a cross-looking old lady. Maybe Miss Fortin just stayed in the room this noon. But when we got in the room and were seated, this woman sat down at Miss Fortin's desk. Two of the boys began fighting, like they do, and she got up real mad and walked fast over to them. She grabbed one boy by his hair and twisted him down in his seat like his arm was a handle. Everybody got real still. I was scared and I could feel my heart. I kept watching the door. Maybe Miss Fortin went home for lunch today and was late getting back.

Then this woman stood in front and said that Miss Fortin had lost her father and she would not be back for the rest of the week. She said, "My name is Mrs. Gunther, and I will not stand for any foolishness. My classes are always known as the best disciplined in the school, and you will be no exception."

I couldn't believe it. Miss Fortin wouldn't leave us like that, no matter what. I loved her. She knew that.

"YOU!" I looked up. Mrs. Gunther was pointing at somebody. I looked around to see who she meant. "Yes, you with the red sweater." I looked down at my red sweater. I could almost see my heart banging through it. Me, what? She must mean me, but what was I supposed to do? "Well?" she said. I had to say something. "Well, what?" was all that I could manage. She came down the aisle in a hurry. Grabbing me by the arm, she dragged me up front and plunked me down in Miss Fortin's chair facing the class. "Daydreaming, I will not tolerate," she said to everyone, "and insolence even less." She turned to me. "You may sit there until you learn to behave." I knew everybody was staring at me even though my head was down. My face felt awful hot and suddenly I had to go to the bathroom. Suppose I should disgrace myself in front of everyone? I would just plain have to die, that's all. Maybe I could make myself invisible, but I couldn't work on it because I had to concentrate to keep from having an accident.

While I was concentrating, Mrs. Gunther passed out yellow lined paper. "For our writing lesson we will all send a letter of sympathy to Miss Fortin," she said, not paying any attention to me. I wasn't to get a piece of paper, and there were so many things I wanted to write to Miss Fortin.

Mrs. Gunther wrote on the board:

Dear Miss Fortin,

We are all very sorry that your father has passed away. Be comforted in knowing that he rests with the Lord Jesus, as we all shall some day.

Very truly yours,

(Your name)

"Copy this in your best penmanship, class," she said. The room was still. While everyone wrote, Mrs. Gunther walked up and down the aisles. All that I could do was watch the big hand on the clock hopping its way from minute to minute.

Ours at home went around smooth. I wondered why the school ones jumped. Once it had been on the wrong time when we got to school and then it started to jump fast to catch up. We had all laughed when Miss Fortin said, "My, today is flying!"

Just then the bell rang for recess. Everyone started for the cloak room, but Mrs. Gunther made them come back and march out, a row at a time. I thought then she would say something to me, but she didn't. I guessed she just didn't want to talk to me, and meant for me to get in line. I figured it might make her madder if I went to the cloak room. Anyway my red sweater was warm enough, so I just got up and went to the end of the line. The front of the line was already starting down the stairs when I went by her.

"YOU!" she said. "Who told you to get in line?" She grabbed my shoulder. I tried to explain, but my mouth just moved and nothing came out.

"Go stand in the cloak room," she said. The cloak room? That was only for real awful things. Only two boys in our room had ever been sent there, and they were real awful boys. I don't even remember walking there, but I remember how dark it was. It must have been that nobody remembered to turn on the lights when the class got their jackets, or maybe Mrs. Gunther didn't tell them to and they were afraid to without her saying, so I guessed I had better not, either.

I stood in the cloak room for a long time. I wished somebody would come, but I hoped they wouldn't too. I finally got tired standing, so I sat down on the floor in the corner. What would I say when she did come back? It was so dark I could hardly see the coat hooks. I didn't know I was crying till I felt the wet on the front of my sweater. Then it was too late to stop. Anyway it felt good. My chest ached from holding it back, and I said it could just go ahead and come, and it did. I knew my eyes were getting all red, but I didn't care.

Then I heard clumpety-clump footsteps, and I knew Mrs. Gunther was coming back. My heart banged. The tears stopped, like shutting off a faucet, but I was shaking. I squeezed down in the corner. The door opened, and "click" the light went on. It hurt my eyes so I put my head down on my knees.

Mrs. Gunther came over and put her hand under my chin and yanked up my head. "Why, you've been crying," she said. She smiled kind of funny with that put-on sweet look that my Aunt Sarah sometimes got. Then she pulled me up and hugged me to the front of her. Her jacket scratched, and she smelled sweaty.

"That's a good girl," she said. "You've learned your lesson now, haven't you? You're going to be a good girl and I'll be like your mother, won't I?" My stomach jumped around, and I was glad I didn't eat much of that fried egg sandwich because I was afraid that if I had, it wouldn't have stayed put.

"You come back to your seat now, Dear," she said, "and we'll wait for the others to come back." I kept my head down when they came in so they wouldn't see I'd been crying. We always went to the art room after recess, and I knew I could ask Miss Manetti to let me go to the bathroom if I could last that long. I did.

That night, Daddy asked me how school went like he always did. I started to say, "O.K." like always, but then I said, "We had a substitute today."

"That's nice, Honey," he said. He was reading the paper and probably had a lot on his mind. Anyway I got a tight feeling inside and was glad he didn't ask any more.

The next morning at breakfast Mrs. Moody said, "Come on, now, eat your egg or you'll miss the bus." I tried to get the egg down, but my stomach was at it again. The first thing I knew all of last night's supper came up.

"For heaven's sakes!" cried Mrs. Moody and sent me to the bathroom to wash my face. While I was there, I heard her say to my father, "It's just put on so she won't have to go to school."

"Nonsense," my father said, "she likes school. Besides, no one can make himself sick. She must have picked up the grippe. A few days in bed will do her good. That's where I went, and I remember I didn't get better until the end of the week.

I looked down at the red sweater in my lap and realized with a start that it looked very much like the sweater my own third grader had worn this morning. I wonder if her "Miss Fortin" knows how important she is. Oh, God, grant her the love of many Miss Fortins that she may have strength for the Mrs. Gunthers,

COMMENT: How insensitive can some people be (even teachers).

Remember this adult mother still had bad memories of this unfortunate day in her childhood so many years before!

THINGS A CHILD MIGHT SAY TO A PARENT

1. My hands are small -- don't expect perfection
2. My eyes have not seen the world -- please let me explore
3. House duties will always be there -- I am little for a short time
4. My feelings are tender -- please don't yell at me
5. I am a special gift from God -- guide me in a loving manner
6. I need encouragement -- tell me what I do RIGHT
7. Give me freedom to make some of my decisions
8. It can be demeaning to do things over for me
9. We may need a vacation from each other -- take time for yourself
10. Go with me to Sunday School and Church regularly

To a child, it often may seem that the three R's are not Reading, 'Riting, 'Rithmetic, but Rules, Routines, and Responsibilities. This may be avoided by setting the guidelines early in the year and expecting good behavior.

It would be well to consider what we hope to accomplish by means of discipline. Each child has his or her own individuality, so expression to the nature of the child should be allowed. It is important to understand the child with the proper attitude to command respect, love and cooperation, a method of leading instead of driving. A wise teacher knows that all children are not alike.

CHAPTER EIGHT
THE WAY OF THE CLASSROOM

FIRST OF THE YEAR MEETING WITH PARENTS

Explanation of Home Study Program

1. It is helpful to review each day what has been taught that day in the school. This reinforces the lesson and repetition is good. Also, the child knows the parent is involved with the learning process. Many comments from parents acknowledged appreciation for this involvement. Encourage your child to ask questions if a concept is not understood. I will explain as often as necessary for understanding. I do not like to encourage students to not listen by tuning out when instruction is given. I think the habit is started in early years of not listening. As the little boy said, "It

was not important, because the teacher only said it one time."

2. Requirements for promotion to Second Grade
3. Finger Counting in math -- a habit very difficult to break once it is started. Better to use sticks or other objects, but not fingers.
4. School rules and field trip information.
5. Working with a child -- stay calm. If frustrated, take a break. AN UPSET CHILD IS NOT LEARNING
6. Remember your child is one of many in a classroom, and the teacher must be fair to the whole class. Many things can be upsetting to the class --

For instance:

Mashed potatoes on new shoes -- child in tears

Ants in lunch boxes -- VERY upsetting

Caught zippers

Late bus -- children coming in and a lunch box fell open

Parental notes turned in late that had been forgotten

Intercom: child in another room was sick and going home -- Brother should not wait after school

Intercom: bookmobile is here -- send class at scheduled time

Child left a book on the bus

Father brought forgotten lunch money -- tear up charge slip

LEAST DESIRABLE TEACHING JOB

BUS DUTY -- about once a month each teacher is scheduled to have Bus Duty. This does not seem to be a problem, but it is before school in the morning when all the children who arrive early are to stay in the lunchroom until class time. There can be considerable exuberance -- meaning joyously unrestrained action. Usually two teachers are teamed up together in this assignment.

After school is a different situation. The students usually wait outside the building if it isn't raining, and watch for the bus to come. After the constraints of the classroom all day, there is often unreleased energy that has to be released. The biggest concern usually are the students from other classrooms who do not know the teacher on duty, and there can be disrespect and sassiness.

We had one bus driver who was well over six feet tall, who also was assistant coach in the High School. I imagine he appeared to the students on the bus as about seven feet tall. He had the students on his bus line up boys in one line and girls in another line and they took turns each day as to which line entered first and took their ASSIGNED seats. There was no running to the bus when they saw it coming. It was considerably different than some of the other buses. I never knew how he got the control he had, but some of the parents complained that he was too strict. I thought it was strange how some parents react, because I thought they should thank him for the safety of their children.

MONTHLY ATTENDANCE REPORT

Every day all absences or any tardiness is recorded, and at the end of the month all this information is compiled with absences marked either excused or unexcused. Then each column is totaled with all totals agreeing. There are several checks to make sure all figures are correct. One teacher in each grade takes turns in compiling all reports for that grade level. I always appreciated the kind notes from parents when they sent in the reason for absence. We were in a very fine school district and the majority of parents were concerned and interested in their children, as I think most parents are, but they have different ways of expressing the concern THE ATTENDANCE REGISTER MUST BE CLEAN AND NEAT! -- black ink only and no white-out used.

LANGUAGE DIFFERENCES

Think of yourself from another country, and try to interpret some of these sentences:

1. The bandage was wound around the wound.
2. The farm was used to produce produce
3. The dump was so full that it had to refuse more refuse
4. The soldier decided to desert his dessert in the desert
5. No time like the present, so it is best to take time present the present
6. The wind was too strong to wind the sail
7. After a number of injections, I felt numbness in my jaw

English is a crazy language. There is no egg in eggplant and no ham in hamburger. There is no apple or pine in pineapple, and why is it called a shipment when it goes by car and a cargo when it goes by ship? So many words or meanings of words can be misunderstood, and a child has all this to learn.

Another word in our reading vocabulary that usually brought snickers from the class was the word "but". I explained that the word they were thinking of was not even spelled the same way. -- it had two "T's" instead of one "T". The child who was reading the word was embarrassed when the other children snickered. Mrs. Dawson experienced the same situation in her class, and told the children that the word they were thinking of was part of their anatomy when they sit, and they sure would look funny if they didn't have one. The two explanations seemed to satisfy and the snickering stopped.

Now think of pairs of words that are spelled differently, but pronounced the same. Examples: their--there, here-hear, some-sum, Dye-die, him-hymn, sale-sail, see-sea. Many of these words can also be either a noun or verb, depending how it is used in a sentence.

The light is dim -- light the candle

Saw the wood -- I saw you cut the wood
Animal hide is tough -- hide me from the others
Pool lap lines are marked -- dogs lap up water -- her lap is just
right for reading to a child
The lists are almost endless

BULLETIN BOARDS

Bulletin boards should either display the work of the children
or have some purpose in teaching.
Ideas: Animal pictures
Hot tips for math: read the problem, think, decide, write
The word's greatest kids learn here
We hear with our ears, but listen with our minds

FIELD TRIPS

All students are required to have parental permits
Trips should be educational in nature
Parents are encouraged to go as chaperones, but some
problems may arise. One parent allowed the group to go
back of Falls where there were slippery rocks, and this was an
absolutely forbidden area, but the children coaxed, and they
were allowed.
Ordinarily each chaperone had ten children in a group

REPORT CARD DAY

Any teacher around students when report cards go home,
has probably seen some with fearful looks. Many parents
criticize grades -- no matter how hard the student had tried.
It is better to encourage a child to have his own ideals than
for parents to push their ideals upon their children. Some
children may need more incentive to study, but I believe that
is something that starts even before the crawling stage. It is

better to comment on the beautiful "A", and what can we do about that "C"? There are many different personalities in each student in attaining scholastic endeavor and adulthood, but constant nagging from parents often accomplishes nothing and often works in reverse to the intended goal.

TEACHER RESPONSIBILITIES

Always good to keep lines of communication open between home and school.

1. Never ask a question: "How many times do I have to tell you?"
2. Not wise to make a prediction
3. Obvious fact statements are not needed, like -- "You are out of your seat." The child knows this.

CHAPTER NINE
IT WORKED FOR ME

ON REACHING UNREACHED CHILDREN

"If you can't love me, at least notice me". I immediately think of a child named Marianne Lollman. She was noticeably not clean and often had a blank look without input in class. I often visited in the home of a child who seemed to be not relating to me. However, I did not get inside Marianne's home, but her mother came out to talk beside the car. Obviously the mother had been drinking, and there was not much accomplished with our discussion, but such a difference it made in Marianne. I saw a beauty in that child's eyes that I had never noticed before and she perked up in class. I had the feeling that she thought if her teacher cared enough about her to come to her home, she must have some value unknown before.

Then there was little Archie Noahs (nicknamed "Ark"). In

his school work, he did not excel, but he was personality plus with a great big smile. He purposely went by each morning to greet the principal with a cheery, "Good morning, Mr. Davis". The principal said that Ark may not learn to read, but he would certainly get along in the world with his personality. He could draw with intricate detail, and the principal's prophetic words were true when his talent was used in vocational tenth grade and he learned body work and repairing of cars. The last I heard he was doing very well financially in his work.

Next I think of a boy named Tom Johnson (called T.J.), who wouldn't talk in school while the other children were there -- even if someone passed by the windows outside. He would read to me after school while waiting for his bus. His mother said he read quite well at home. One day in reading group, the children were saying words from flash cards and if they missed a word, they would go to the end of the circle chairs. To the amazement of the teacher and students, T.J. said the word rather than go to the circle end. After that, his oral speaking improved.

Another child, Elsie Galvin, started crying for no apparent reason and could not seem to get her mind on her class work. Finally in private she told me that she was having to leave because her parents were moving. In getting the whole story from her mother who taught at the same school I found out that she was adopted and had been in several foster homes. Every time her foster parents moved, she was sent to another foster home. Of course that got straightened out in a hurry when her adoptive parents knew she was so concerned. A teacher's heart aches for some of the problems that children have to handle.

RULE ON THINGS BEING TRADED

Many small things like pencils and even larger items attract a child's attention. They may ask the child for the item, and think they have a trade for something the other child agrees to trade. Then the first owner changes his or her mind and wants it back. I found one way to handle it was there was NOT a trade until I had a note from parents of both children giving permission for the trade.

TELEPHONE CALLS

It was my opinion a telephone in each room would be a great help, and I think that is getting to be the custom in many schools. If there is not one, I found it to be very helpful to call the parents on my time and discuss anything of need. A record of these calls was kept with the date, reason for the call, who I had talked with, and any solution.

A BIG HELP FOR MISBEHAVIOR NOT SEEN BY TEACHER

It is never wise to accuse a child of something he or she had done without seeing it. A solution that was VERY HELPFUL was to have the child go to the back of the room and write exactly what had taken place or what had been said. (This was mostly with third graders). Then what was written would be read by the child to the class. Without comment, the heads of the other children would acknowledge what was read. Children all seem to know what has gone on. If the heads were shaking "No", the child would rewrite. Sometimes it would take three or four tries, but eventually the writer seemed to decide it had to be written as to what had really happened. When the heads nodded up and down, we knew we had the whole story.

After the paper was signed, the child was told it would be filed in my desk and if the incident happened again, it would come out either to the principal or to the parents. Most of the time the problem was handled. I preferred handling it at school than with the parents.

Some notes written by a child show there are usually two

sides to every story, so I think it is always wise for a teacher to not make accusations without seeing what actually happened. Some notes follow:

"I will never squeal in the rest room again. I am sorry what I did. I hope you will not catch me again."

"I was up at the garbage can with my pencil sharpener. Then Virgil came, and I was getting something when he was bent down and when he leaned up, I stepped over and by accident kicked him in the foot. Then he started to kick me and went to tell the teacher."

"I said a bad word when the teacher stepped out of the classroom. The teacher put my name on the chalkboard and made me write you this letter. P.S. I will not say that word again."

"I tore Ark's shirt last Thursday. We were playing a game and he told some other people and me to chase him and tag him on the shoulder. I did. He kept going and I was fixing to let go and my hand got caught in his shirt and tore it, and then I said I was sorry."

"I was walking by Marianne -- she was walking too. I have a sore throat and I got some spit in my mouth. I was trying not to hit her and spit behind her, but accidentally spit on her."

(Other child's response) "That's not true. I was walking to the room from washing the tables. (Boy's name) looked right at me and spit on me."

"I was walking from music and Ellie was walking slow. I was passing her, and stepped too quickly and accidentally hit her in the stomach."

(Ellie's response) I was walking on the sidewalk and Virgil took his elbow and hit me in the stomach and pushed me off the sidewalk."

A SICK CHILD

We were fortunate to have a clinic with volunteer mother gray ladies who took turns being at the school during the school day. If a child was feeling ill or had a fever, he or she was sent to the clinic with a note as to the problem. The gray ladies could let the child rest a short time and determine if the child needed to have parents called to come, or could be returned to the class after resting.

During the course of my teaching years I had several children who were diabetic. Whenever a diabetic child put his or her head down on the desk, it signaled a diabetic coma. In my desk I had several packages of unopened crackers and this usually would arouse the child as it was probably near lunch time, and then I would walk holding the child's hand to lunch.

SUBJECT MATTER

READING - phonetic principles. Like all teaching methods, some children learn one way and other children learn by another method. Phonics is so important in beginning reading instruction. Often rules are very helpful.

1. First learn the a,e,i,o,u vowels, and sometimes y and w
2. All words have at least one vowel -- establish the long and short vowel sounds.
   DRILL, DRILL, DRILL
3. When two vowels are in a word, the first one is usually long
4. One vowel in a word is USUALLY short
5. One vowel at the end of a short word is USUALLY long
6. Some groups of two letters are pronounced as one sound

It is important to use the word USUALLY, because there are exceptions to every rule in our language. Of course comprehension is very important, but if the phonetic principles are not started at the beginning reading time, it is difficult to teach them after the child has gotten his or her own method of reading.

Also, it is important to be aware that each child may have different needs in the way he or she learns -- some by hearing, some by sight, some by doing, and some by hands on.

WRITING IDEAS

A child will usually only write as neatly as it is required or expected. One child who had trouble writing neatly brought a paper to the teacher, and when the teacher asked what it said, he said, "How should I know? I can't read it." That can be an attitude if neat writing is not required. You can probably imagine the answer to that question when he had to do his work over.

Some suggestions for when the class can write their own subjects:

1. What is special about me?
2. What makes me feel happy? Lonely? Excited? Scared?
3. Write what you really care about
4. Write something that is important to you

Have the class think about organizing their thoughts -- first, second, last

STATE BOOKLETS

Toward the end of the year the third graders chose a state and made a booklet with six pages. All this was done in the classroom, and not just assigned to do at home. Material was available for them to write four paragraphs about the state they had chosen. I gave them the first line of each paragraph to get them started, and they were to complete the page.

One page was an outline of the state, another page a picture of the state's flag and another page of the state flower. The pictures were either drawn or traced and colored. We also put on a cover page with the pertinent information. I felt it was important to give the help in the classroom and not expect parents to do it at home. I had many notes of appreciation from parents about this practice. In grading, each page was given so many points as to how neatly it was done. This gave room for creativity and expertise in drawing, coloring and neatness.

Page 1 -- Title page
Page 2 -- Report and sources -- 50 points
Page 3 -- State outline -- 5 points
Page 4 -- State bird picture -- 15 points
Page 5 -- State flower picture -- 15 points
Page 6 -- Flag picture -- 15 points

We also made similar booklets on Presidents and Symbols of Freedom. As a beginning sentence, I would sometimes get them started with something like: "There are several symbols that represent freedom in the United States. One of these symbols is the _____ (whatever the child chose to write about)

PRESIDENT BOOKLET

Page 1 -- Title page
Page 2 -- Report and 2 sources -- 50 points
Page 3 -- Oath of office -- 20 points
Page 4 -- Presidential seal -- 30 points

SYMBOLS OF FREEDOM

Page 1 -- Title page
Page 2 -- Report and 2 sources -- 50 points

Page 3 -- Liberty Bell -- 10 points
Page 4 -- Statue of Liberty -- 10 points
Page 5 -- Bald Eagle -- 10 points
Page 6 -- Great Seal -- 10 points
Page 7 -- Flag -- 10 points

It is difficult for a child to complete an assignment when not knowing how to get started, and most children want to do what is expected if they are just told how to do it. This also is preparation for later years when they are given term paper assignments.

Several writing subjects that were most enlightening were what the child expected in the new grade. Some reasons were:

"I am going to like learning. My friend told me that my teacher was nice. I am going to like my teacher, and am happy being in this room. My favorite subject is math. What I like about school is the P.E. I got four brothers and I love them. I lost a tooth last night."

"I like third grade, but we will have hard work. My favorite subject is spelling. I do not like language. I like the desk the best because it is bigger than last year. I like to play with my dog -- his name is Mickey and he is white. My mother is nice and pretty."

"School is going to be fun. I am happy to be in this room. I like all subjects. I have a brother that is a pest. I have one brother. I hope I have a friend. My brother had a bike wreck."

"My grandmother had breast surgery. She had five operations. I wanted to be in your class. Today I have to go to day care and then I got to go somewhere."

"I would like to know how to tell time. I wanted to be in this room. I want you to know that I am sometimes bad and sometimes good. I didn't like my other school last year. I think the teachers are better here than my other school."

"I expect cursive writing and I would like to do times. I would not like to be bad in class. Me and my mother got a new car. I bet I will have lots of friends this year. My sister has a black eye. We think she fell off the bed and bumped her eye. I'm glad you are my teacher. I want to learn some things so when I grow up I will not be dumb."

HOMEWORK ASSIGNMENTS

Much of a teacher's time is in checking homework. I felt there were more important things to do with my time in teaching the children. At the first of the year I asked parents to check over their child's work that had been done at home. I chose to NOT give homework on weekends and told the class that was my choice.

In my desk I had a folder for each child. First thing in the morning the papers were to come in and placed in the folders. They were in alphabetical order and the children soon knew when they were next to turn the paper in. It only took a very few minutes. At a glance I could see if the child understood what had been done. The class was told if an assignment was not turned in, there would be a note written on the folder with the date and the reason given for not turning in the assignment. The goal was to have no notes written on the folder for uncompleted work. A line was drawn at the end of the six weeks period, and a new six weeks started with no uncompleted notes on it. There was no scolding to the child, and actually a very few comments had to be written.

These folders could be shown during a parent conference, if needed.

BATHROOM PERMISSION

It was a policy in the room that a child did NOT have to interrupt the class by asking to go to the restroom. They were told if they abused that policy, they would have to ask before going. We had an adjoining rest room, and that worked very well.

CLASS PLAYS

Knowing from experience that at the end of the year and the week before Christmas holidays, there is not really much learning that goes on in the classroom. For several years I started having the children do little plays those two weeks. During the year, the class had worked hard so we were able to accomplish what was needed for their grade level. As a type of reward for their hard work, all books were collected, tests completed, and full attention given to little plays.

At Christmas, I chose to NOT use a Biblical theme, because often it is done with a tinge of comedy, and I did not want that aspect. The thought was to give several short plays, so every child had a part, and if possible a speaking part. There was no pressure for memorization or costuming. If the child wanted to bring something from home to wear, it was good, and if the speaking part was memorized, that was fine, but not required. I wanted the least burden for parents as possible, and it was amazing what children can do on their own as third graders. Some of the plays we did were Mouse-Deer, The Trial of Mother Goose, Miss Louisa and the Outlaws, The person Downstairs, and the Three Bears. Usually one child would be the announcer or the story-teller. Some of our plays came from our readers, and often class singing was incorporated in the play.

It was a very rewarding experience and amazing what they achieved. One end-of-the-year note from a boy said, "This year of school was fun and not fun. The fun things were P.E. and Plays." It was not the plan to choose the best students for the outstanding parts, but often just the opposite. However, every student was in an important part. This was a busy hub of activity, and we invited other classes a few at a time to join us as the audience, and also did the plays for the parents the last day of school.

ASSESSMENT NOTE TO PARENTS

Note sent home with the report card asking how the parents and child were responding to the school program.

Name of child _____

Home study going well _____ Yes _____No

Having some difficulty _____ Yes _____ No

Suggestions or Comments _____

Many nice comments were received, and it gave a better assessment of the classroom environment for the students.

CLASS EQUIPMENT

Puzzles were always to be kept in the puzzle holder, and if a child could not complete the puzzle, all pieces were to be put on top of the puzzle and placed on the teacher's desk. Then another child would get the puzzle and put it together. In all my years, I only had two pieces lost and that was when a new student came into the room, and did not know the system. He put the puzzle back not completed, and the janitor probably swept up the pieces on the floor. A kind father made pieces on his jig-saw to fit the puzzle.

In all the work of a teacher, it is important to keep attitudes in the positive, and not in the negative. A child soon knows if the teacher cares for the students, or if it is just a job. A principal was taking the pay checks to the rooms for each teacher. A little boy questioned the teacher as to when she worked, because she was always there with the class. Ah, yes!

There is a difference in "Rigidity" and "Flexibility". Children definitely need to know their guidelines. Most children (not all) try to please adults and a child is more creative if all decisions are not made for him or her. It helps greatly to have support and kind notes from parents just to know that work with their child is being appreciated.

In closing this chapter, I am reminded of a young boy who climbed up on the cabinet when I went out of the room for a short time. He threatened to the class that he was going to jump off. He was still on the cabinet when I returned. My response was, "Don't you EVER get on the cabinet when I am out of the room. If you have to do it, do it when I am in the room, so I can catch you!" He never tried it again.

CHAPTER TEN
THEN AND NOW

BIG CHANGES HAVE BEEN MADE

There is no question in anybody's mind who has been around a few years and is aware of what if going on in the schools, that society and society's children have changed in their behavior. A few years ago, teachers described the top seven problems in the school classroom were talking, chewing gum, making noise, running in the halls, improper dress, waste paper not being placed in the waste paper basket, and now it is more like rape, robbery, assault, burglary, arson, bombing and murder!! There is a decadence in moral and spiritual training, and it seems lying is often NOT considered as a sin unless the liar gets caught. The power to turn this tide in America and the world is for Bible-believing Christians to take a stand in the schools and in families.

School officials are being hand-cuffed in the teaching

of spiritual morals. It is true that we as a nation are under severe attack of the adversary, the Devil. At thanksgiving time I asked the students to memorize the 100th Psalm and recite it in front of the class. Parents all thanked me for the assignment -- all except one mother. She objected and to my surprise, the family was a church-going family. The objection came at Open House, and I told the mother if she didn't want her daughter memorizing the Psalm, to pick out some other poem about Thanksgiving. This she did and the students all wondered why she did not recite the Psalm, but some other poem. I just told them that her mother wanted her to learn the poem.

This is a note I received from the child's mother. Our daughter has tried her best to learn this poem even though she has had only one night to do so. I trust you are not giving her only one day to learn this new poem as punishment for not wanting to learn the Bible verse. It was the mother who did not want her to learn the Psalm, and it was ridiculous to say she had only one night to learn the poem.

Another time the same mother wrote that the child was too hot in the room. Most children were wearing light sleeveless clothing and this child would come in long socks, heavier clothing and sweaters. Some people just seem to like something to complain about and do not realize the teacher is their child's friend. Perhaps she couldn't find anything to complain about.

It is very disturbing for the school to get blamed for many of the problems in the schools. I have always felt that the schools are a mirror of society and when parents recognize it is their responsibility to train their children in moral and spiritual values along with manners and honesty, perhaps some of the problems will be turned around.

It has been suggested that one week be set aside during which teachers would teach their routine classes and nothing extra be added; during that week there would be no class meetings for the teacher, no tests, no yearbook or ring sales, no pictures taken, no assemblies, no field trips, no school fair, no play rehearsal, no art festival, no eye testing, no fire drill, no pep rally, no TB skin testing, no open-house, or no holiday. Perhaps if we could do that, students might be able to do what they are supposed to do in school -- LEARN, and teachers could to what they are supposed to do -- TEACH!

After the Christmas vacation there had been a visit of some unknown person who caused a lot of vandalism in the school. My room showed all the letter cards down from the wall with the edge of one burned and lying on the cabinet. Another was dirty and in the trash can, three cabinet doors were standing open, the desks were tipped over, candy wrappers were on the floor, teacher desk lock was broken and all in disarray, scratch marks on the desk top, a present that had been given to a child who was absent before vacation had been opened and gone, all the registration cards had been gone through to see who was in the room. What a mess!

In another room there was a similar mess with trash from the outside trash cans scattered throughout the room and on the grass outside. It was determined in that room that a janitor who had been befriended by that teacher in getting the job for him had become disgruntled because he was no longer to work there. His idea of cleaning the rest rooms was to go in and flush the commodes. His work was just not satisfactory, so he took it out on her. Later he was heard to say that now it was a lot better because he could sit on the porch and watch for his check to come in the mail -- No work!

Then there was the child who was transferring from a private school and the mother raved about how far ahead the little girl was and the exceptional instruction she had received at the former school. After working with the little girl a short time, I realized she was one reading level behind my lowest group. How do you tell a parent of this situation without putting them into shock?

The lunchroom supervisor sent a note home inviting the parents to have lunch with the child for the Thanksgiving Dinner. The menu was to be baked turkey, cornbread dressing, pimento cheese stuffed celery, green beans almondine, hot rolls, ice cream and cookie, milk with coffee or tea for adults. Great menu and very accommodating to invite the parents, but most of the children carried their lunch on that day because they are not accustomed to that type of food. Many children prefer fast food -- like hot dogs, hamburgers, pizza, etc.

One large boy who had tried to commit suicide in kindergarten said his favorite food was chocolate-covered french fries.

Another child had no resemblance to letters in his writing. One day I took time to show and help him and he made some beautiful letters. He then put out his hand to be punished. My! My! It showed what the child had expected and the influence of a teacher at just the right time, but certainly not one for the child to be punished.

A little girl had a young bunny and said that she was going to bring rabbits to school and sell them free -- she said you know how they multiply.

TESTING

Tests do take a lot of time that could be good teaching time. Do better scores really mean better learning? Although I have thought for years that tests were not the best approach, there has to be some method in this day and time to assess the student's progress -- especially in the older children, and I don't have a better solution. I do think one big answer is having competent, conscientious teachers and instilling in young children a desire to learn and do their best.

There was a time for the very young child that grades were not given on report cards. There would be a teacher assessment like "Excellent", "Good", "Needs work", "Student trying" without the discouraging A,B,C's to a child who is really trying. Liability is a big problem now, and there has to be a reason shown for any grade that is given.

MERIT PAY

My first thought is who is going to make the deciding factor as to which teachers get the extra pay?

1. Would the students, other teachers, principal, parents, test scores be the unbiased deciding factor?
2. Many cultural differences in language and ability of the children make a difference
3. Many emotional problems in the class that must be handled
4. There may be less than a helpful attitude between teachers knowing that some will receive merit pay and some will not.

A TEACHER WHO TRIES TO DO THE BEST TEACHING IN ANY SITUATION COULD NOT BE DOING ANY BETTER WITH AN INCENTIVE OR MERIT PAY

Also, at one time the day started with a Bible story, the Lord's Prayer in unison, then the Pledge of Allegiance and the singing of America. Before leaving for the lunchroom, the class offered thanks for their food. One day a little boy wanted to say the blessing for us, and this is what he said, "God is great, God is good. We pray that our food will not have poison and be sweet and good."

This is not necessarily under the caption of testing, but one day the third grade teachers were asked to review a film on human development before showing it to the children. After comments were given to the principal about the film, this is the note that went home to the parents. "After the teachers previewed the film on human development, they do not think it is a good idea to show this film to your children.

They believe it is too advance for 8 and 9 years old."

Zowie!! Today younger children then 8 and 9 probably see films much more advanced than that one on television every day. Former dangers were open fireplaces, wringer washers, cisterns and wells, typhoid fever, polluted drinking water, old refrigerator traps, or kerosene lamps. No! No! We don't want to go back to those problems, but we certainly are creating new problems in our children with television, movies, computers, and an indifferent attitude in the rearing of the generation that will be taking over the world in a few years.

SITUATIONS OF INTEREST

There was a child who showed a lack of security and often lied. At one time she took lunchroom tickets from the teacher's desk, and then had to talk to the principal about what she had done. Her attitude seemed to change when she realized she was trying to be helped, not just punished. Later she told the truth about being in the teacher desk and wanted to know why I was so proud of her for telling the truth. Her mother was an alcoholic and whenever the teacher got close to the child, she would grab the teacher's hand. (Some children have so many emotional needs.)

In writing his actions, a child said, "I was running around when I was supposed to be lining up at P.E. The P.E. teacher jerked my arm and put her face real close to mine. It hurt my arm." (Question) How long did it hurt? (Child) "about two minutes", and he thought his parents would be ready to sue the P.E. teacher, the school and the Board of Education. Another child offered the advice that the teacher could be sued if there was a red mark.

Before school a little boy was playing catch with his lunch and it landed on the outside roof. Another boy trying to help threw his paste jar up to knock it down, and it also landed on the roof. When the principal came into the room, the teacher told him that the boy had something to tell him. The child started crying and couldn't talk, so he was told to go outside and show the principal what had happened. All was well when the janitor came in with the lunch and paste jar -- both boys were very relieved. (It is my opinion that there are many ways of handling incidents without scolding and punishing.)

FLAT STATEMENTS OF STUDENTS

(Last days of school) -- "I'm going to have some days off."

In Phonics, child was asked how many vowels in the word "His". The child said "three". Teacher reminded the vowels are A,E,I,O,U. The child then said there was one vowel. When asked if the vowel was long or short. The child said it was short because The "S" makes the "H" long. Can be confusing to a child, can't it?

(Another child) - "We'll go to Heaven and grow bones. God turns bad people into witches -- like my mother!"

"Somebody stole my pencil!" (Found on the floor under the desk)

Teachers are often also guilty of making flat statements, but the commonest one is, "I've had it!"

Then the question often is why should I continue to be or want to be a teacher? Education is losing valued teachers to better paying jobs and having constant homework and paperwork to do. It is one of the hardest jobs there is, if a teacher really tries to do it right.

ADVICE TO EDUCATION BOARDS

Improve, don't prolong the school day. The year it was necessary to have two classes share a room with a class in the morning, and the other class from 12:00 to 4:00 -- even with two teachers. A lot was accomplished that may not have been improved by being there longer. Quality of teaching is not improved by longer class time. Then as we have heard, "Thank goodness businessmen don't teach!" Many things would just not be put up with that are required of teachers. And again -- the main thing is "AND TEACH, TOO!"

This note from a mother was appreciated: "I did not know that (child) brought a sling-shot to school. I do not approve of him bringing any toys to school, especially not a sling-shot. He no longer has a sling-shot. Thank you for telling about his misbehavior.

REFRESHING PRINCIPAL BULLETINS

A good principal will try to keep memos in the positive as our principal did. On one bulletin after asking teachers to be in their rooms at 7:45 on a work day and be at the school at 7:30, there were seven other instructions. The last one was: "Turn in money, and go home." Another said, "We had a good first semester. I hope the second one will be good also. Thank you."

One note in the before school in-service meeting said, "No meetings today -- all teachers can work in their rooms. (What a relief!)

"Just a note to wish you a Merry Christmas and a Happy New Year. We have had a good year and you have helped make it possible.

The poem: "Merry Christmas to all and to all a good night." "I want this year to end with this thought -- Merry Christmas to all and to all a good two weeks vacation. See you next year, and thanks (Signed)

How the teachers did appreciate our principal's backing and helpfulness -- he was great!

CONCLUSION

As Henry Adams once said, "A teacher affects eternity. He can never tell where his or her influence stops." So very true!! Another quote from a teacher who was retiring after forty years in the teaching profession, "I give God the glory if I have been able to help a single child or colleague." Sacrifices are made that most people would never imagine. Teachers can get blamed for everything that is wrong and often little credit for what is right.

Along with these statements, there are also many rewards. A great big reward is working to explain a concept and it seems the children are not understanding, and all of a sudden it is obvious when you see a light bulb come on in the child's face that what has been explained has finally been understood.

Another reward is when the children send such meaningful, precious notes expressing their love for their teacher and how much they have learned. They also draw pictures and even though the pictures may not resemble the teacher, they put a big smile on the face in their drawing. That means a lot.

SOME RESPONSES RECEIVED

"I want to use this opportunity to let you know how much (child) has loved and enjoyed you this year, and we have been very pleased with his work and his learning this year."

"I have had lots of teacher, but you are the best. LOVE, (Child)

"I like you very much, I like how you teach me. You are

the best teacher in the world. You are the smartest teacher all around because you know what you are doing, and you are very careful. I think you are so nice to me every day. It seems you are nicer every day." Love (Child)

"I am glad to be in your class this year. I asked if you could be my teacher at the office and they said yes. Merry Christmas.

"I love you. I wish you were a second grade teacher"

"I would like to thank you for making this a very enjoyable school year. You are the kind of teacher every parent and child hopes for; -- strict, but fair, fun, and a God-given talent for teaching. You will go down in our book as the best teacher (Child) has had. We wish you much happiness.

"(Child's name), Dad and I would like to thank you for the superb job that you are doing. We would especially thank you for the time and effort that you take to keep us informed on our child's progress. I am aware of how time-consuming this can be -- especially with 32 students in a class. I can see that study habits have been established that will be needed for the rest of the school years. Many students go through school and never really learn how to study or to take responsibility to prepare for the next day's assignment. To learn this is a milestone in one's education process and I believe that (child) is getting the foundation for this now.

In short, your efforts are appreciated and we thank God for gifted teachers who are sincerely interested in children. Thanks again

(Signed by both parents)

"(Child) was so excited about make the A-B honor roll. We are very proud of her and are so pleased with her progress over the year. Your encouragement has had a great deal to do with that, and we thank you. It was so great to hear (child) say she felt so good inside and that she was proud of herself.

Sincerely,

Many times this year I have meant to sit down and write a short note of appreciation about specific things, but my actions have not been as good as my intentions. It is truly a blessing when your children have a teacher who teaches so much more than reading, writing, and arithmetic. It has been a joy to watch (Child) grow and learn this year. I have seen qualities strengthen in her which I know, without doubt, were a direct outgrowth of what you were teaching at school. Thank you for using day-to-day circumstances to teach kindness, honesty, and a caring attitude toward others. You will never know how much it has meant to us for I believe with all my heart that these things will stay with her the rest of her life. God has truly blessed my children with good teachers, who have cared enough to take the time to give them what they needed. Thank you again for using the gift that God has given you to be the teacher you are. Have a nice summer and may God bless you and yours in a very special way. Sincerely,

SUCH A REWARD FOR THE EXPRESSIONS OF CHILDREN AND PARENTS.

I cannot think of anything like money or fame that could surpass such recompense.

Good discipline can be the result of cooperation with the teacher and parents. It can be obtained voluntarily and involuntarily. Involuntary cooperation is accomplished by arousing a fearful attitude and a negative approach, which often leads to sneaking and cheating on part of the students. Voluntary cooperation comes when the teacher is a leader and not a disciplinarian. When the teacher is fair and considerate and admits when making mistakes there will be a more harmonious attitude in the classroom.

Every child needs LOVE, SECURITY, ACCEPTANCE, FAITH, CONTROL, INDEPENDENCE, PROTECTION, SELF-ESTEEM, CONFIDENCE

Dorothy Stebbins Mackey

NOTHING IN THIS WORLD IS AS PRECIOUS AS A
LITTLE CHILD.

About the Author

The author is a graduate student with a Bachelors Degree from Cincinnati Bible College and a Masters in Religion from Butler University in Indianapolis, Indiana -- also a Masters in Guidance Counseling from the University of Alabama in Tuscaloosa, Alabama.

She and her husband, Howard Mackey, have been married for fifty-eight years in November of 2005, and now involved in Music Evangelism. They have three daughters, five grandchildren, and one great grandson.

Three previous books are:

The New Testament Pertaining to Marriage
Memoirs and Thoughts of a Mother
In the Fullness of God's Plan